EARTH TALKING

Poetry Using Images of Nature

Illustrated and Written By

FLORA FENNIMORE

Cover Art, Interior Art, and Poetry are all original work from the author, Flora Fennimore.

All inquiries should be addressed to:

CMP Publishing Group, LLC
27657 Highway 97
Okanogan, WA 98840

EARTH TALKING may be ordered from CMP Publishing Group, LLC, at the above address and at www.cmppg.com.

EARTH TALKING is also available at Amazon.com.

Contact Publisher for distributor information.

email: cmppg@cmppg.com
website: www.cmppg.com

ISBN13: 978-0-9619407-1-3

Library of Congress Control Number: 2010928363

For Ed

CONTENTS

SINGING THE SUN

FINGERING LOVE

QUIVERING ON THE INSIDE

SINGING THE SUN

Illusion

For May day
she wanted a flower
from my roaster pot garden.
I had hoped for days
that the single bud
could feel the resonance
of my anxiety.

No! No! Don't pick it—
it's only half flower!
The slight tremor does not
hold the wind.
It's a butterfly clothing
the bloom.
A flutter ago,
in rhythm to your approach,
it unfurled its wings
and gently back-stroked into
petals of color.
Then, ever so timidly,
it eased its torso,
underside bare,
into soft folds of pollen.
Frame thus settled,
it wove its hold resolutely
onto fibrous sepals.

The gift viewed,
serenity prevailed
...and aspired
when half her gift
soundlessly
lifted into flight.

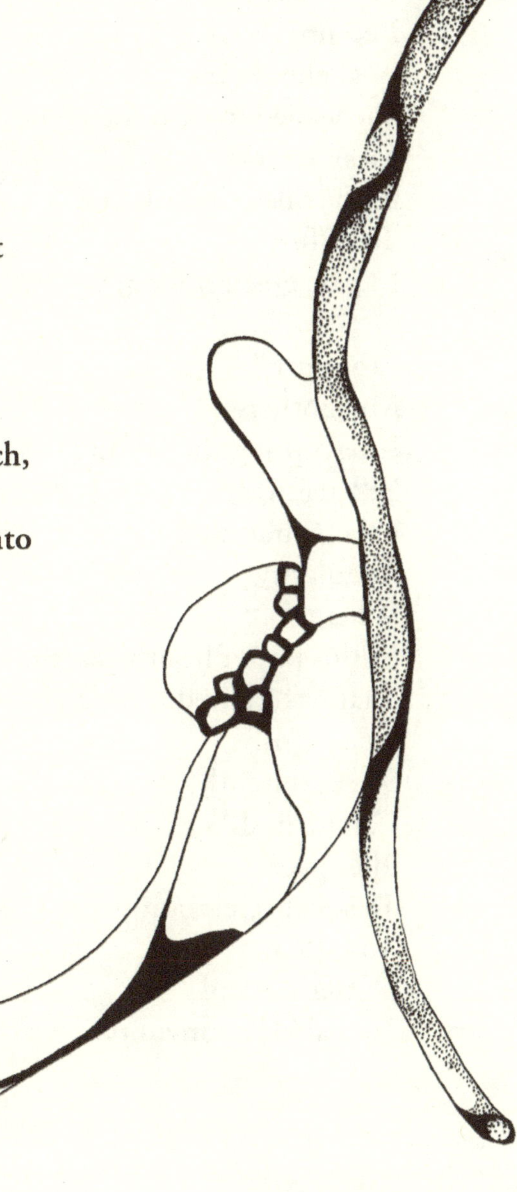

Potted Plant

Expectantly…
Receptively…
In alleluia stance,
She leaned toward the plant
Mesmerizing
Each coiled tendril
To unfurl
In pale green soliloquy.

"Your cat,"
My mother—
Interrupting the gesture—
Yelled at me,
"Has sublime
Angularity.
Where,
In this pot of healthy earth,
That has spewed forth
Ficus brush
So exorbitantly,
Can he find
The space
To squat so elegantly
And, then,
Flutter the soil
To seal his anonymity?"

MOTHER GOOSE
HUMPTY DUMPTY
CREAM
KEIKO
Hissssst!! How cheesy, you plebeian!
the K. Star
COMPOST
Mother's Plant

She Sits

inside a
cage of poppies
daring hinder-posturing
bees to attend.
Rumpling pollen
into the softness
of angel drool,
she fan-traces
irrational beams
into whimsey
feather-flicking
her seeing.
Out of the imagism
comes a hazy
vision
in eight-footed
tap dance.
Ebony hairs magnify
a cyclonic infusion
absently weaving
pollen
into a burnished motley.
Slam-dunking,
the interloper hinges
onto the edge
and reels away
not having stippled
a petal.

Sputum

The sea
spits out
her wealth
in gallant rushes
of breath.

A sand dollar,
it is,
this time.

So pasty pale,
this gritty disk
surprises
with its touch.

Does
it
encourage
the water's sandy
edge?

On
its back
it wears
mail
made of pores—

As if a
stylus,
sharp,
punctured lines,
precise
and concentric,
for the waters
to probe.

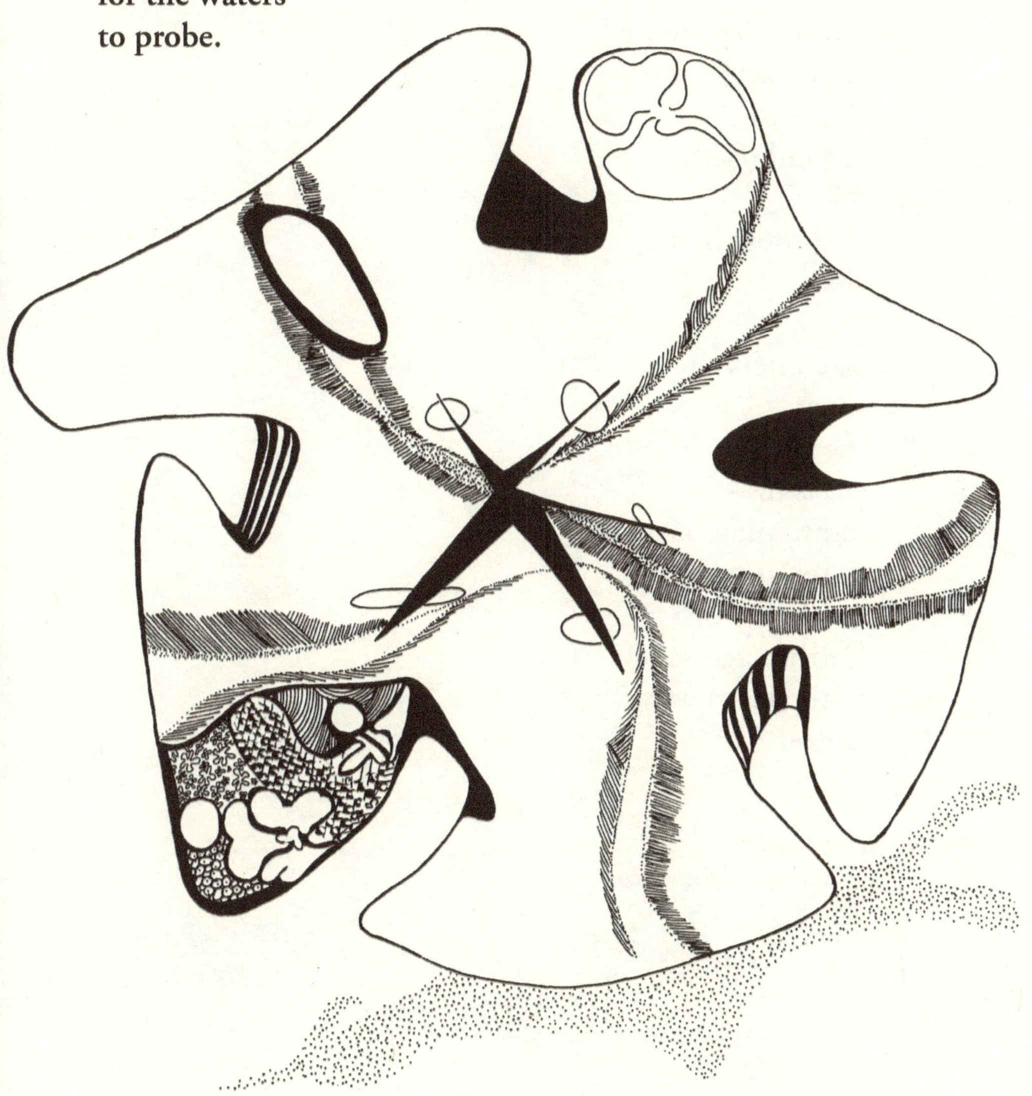

Does it
find
the sea's musing
terse or
buoyant?

Timid
and shallow-footed
it blankets
the sand
around itself
and,
absorbing being,
sits.

The interval
spent,
the sea
sucks in—
in gripping licks—
to reclaim
her crusty orb
for the succession
of the lustrous
dance.

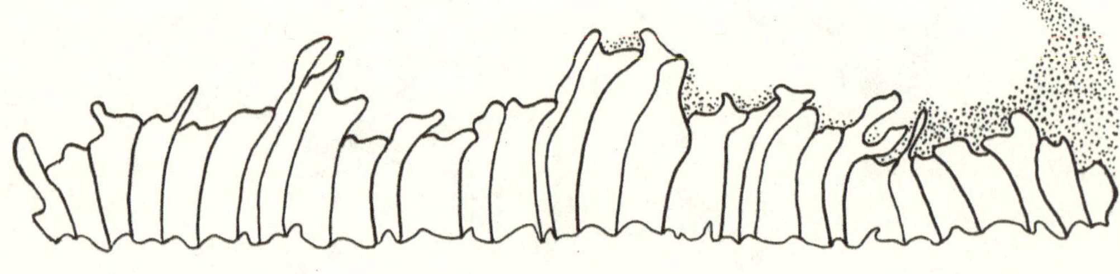

Sing the Sun

The grape vines ride the hill
like a train heading into the valley—
a valley of quilting, pieces pasted
precisely in lettuce spring green
and aubergine washed tomato.
Unseen but felt, the upside-down
river, pulling its path over itself,
talks the silence of plenty. Sun,
squatting behind the wily vines,
tickles the Santa Lucias into a
convoluted embarrassment of
colors, some so dimpled they
hide in their own recesses.

In this scene, I am a squatter
caught without adequate dressing.
In nakedness, the sun
owns my color print
urging me, with crimson accent,
in the ways of the inchworm—
chew your way into safety,
camouflaging mien to the wealth
of greens and flowers well rent.

An Evening Walk

the fog
exhaling filmy language
and fingering low spaces,
suffused the creek
with hosannas

ever persuading,
it countered,
softly swirling
and munching the air

finally,
separating even the sight of us,
except for handclasps,
it mixed with night shade
and swallowed itself

High Desert Remains

Sculpin-mouthed,
clouds of the high desert
belly-squat on skin of sky.
The sun behind them bending
their attitude, they
arch-step moon
now slinking
from nocturnal myth-making
into a cumulus of wantonness.

Turgid…
hunkering on edge
in a swarm of electric beads…
the clouds abandon themselves
to
their own mythic crawls.
Excessively,
they maneuver
wafting altocumulus and
cumulonimbus into a
peasant's poem of desire.

Images, these…
of the high desert…
massage the want
of that soil.….
.….leaving the red blood
smear of Daedalian clouds.

These memories remain…
and our love.

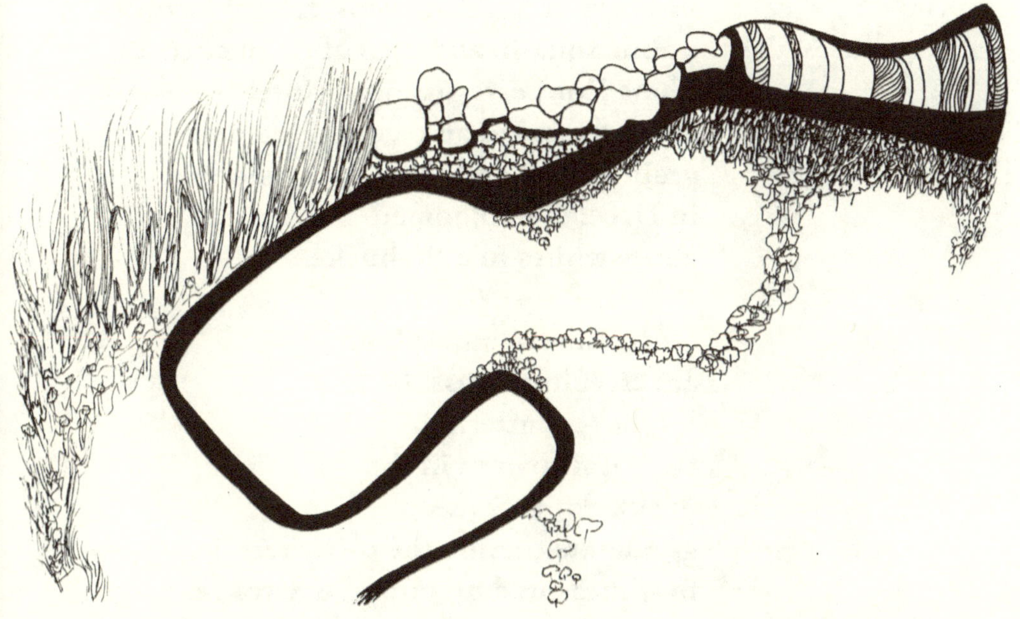

Garden Fugue

I prayed seeds this summer.
From several fists full,
about the size of a softball,
rapacious vines and oracular bushes
squeezed my vegetable plot.
Even the sycophant, Ophelia,
the gopher, chewed up mountains
of pulverized soil to obfuscate her thievery.
Now, I catch my breath in a hobo sack
as the world shuts down in fetal leavings.
Green force had foddered the pith of
  meaning
into jars of braided beans, freezer bags of
nubile squash, and cans of dried cherries.
These icons carry us into winter the way
my dad seamed an oak log into a fine
grain of heat and the way my mother,
in December, bloomed
paper whites in a tin bucket.

Once more, cloud sylphs
are creeping across the hills,
fog shirts fluttering,
faces transparent in the
dusky skies overhead,
gumboots cursing the rocky terrain
foot-measured by Junipero Serra years ago.

FINGERING LOVE

The Moon, My Girl, and Flowers

that night
she came
onto our rock
a shudder
of gentleness
stilled into breathless silence
as the moon
sliced the darkness

pantomiming our mood
we became
two fireflies
fluttering
dipping
settling
molding ourselves into our space

accompanied
by the video of the moon
we recited
"...but I told you...
flowers—miracles of
flowers—for
my birthday..."
she stretched her
arms into an exuberance
of want

at home
with an echo of moon
I took my pad
and entered my garden
there, I drew her
a riot of blossoms
and
with the abandon
of cupid gone awry
I heaved them at her door

the next night
as we came
onto our rock
shyly
pirouetting
effusing the aura
of honey suckle
we touched our way
into a kiss
soft as the lemon chiffon
of the moon

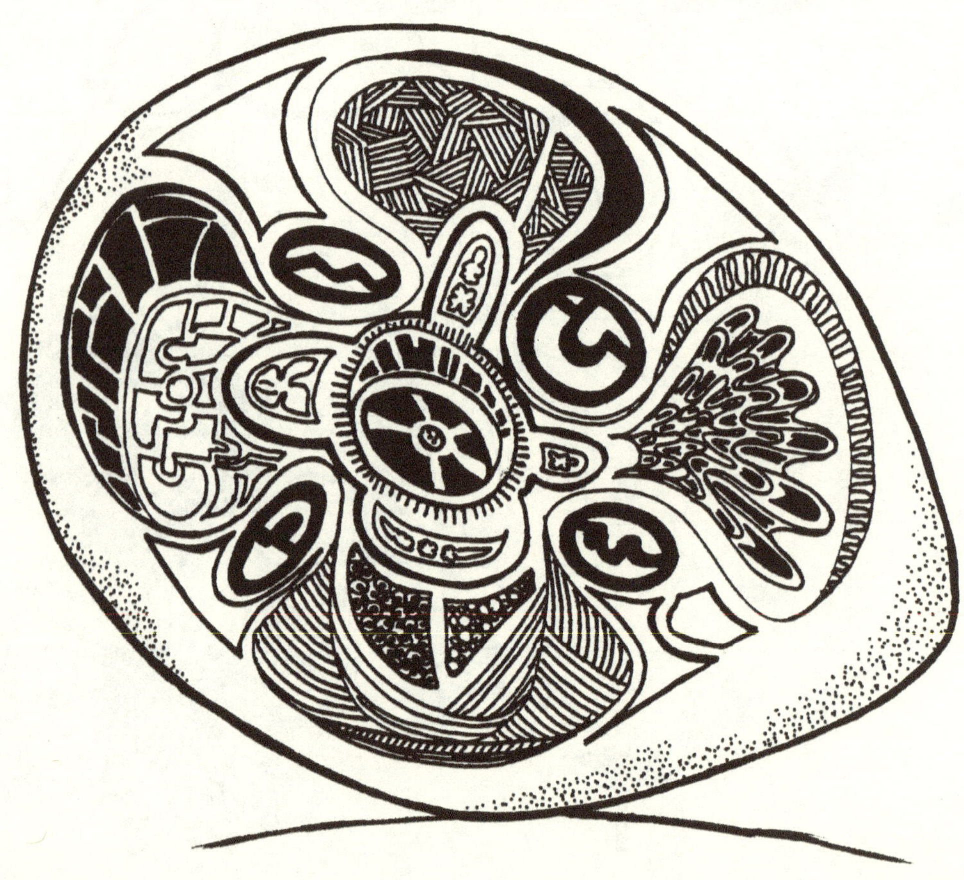

You Are Gone

There it sits—
the Easter egg
you colored in beet root
and onion skins
and fingered
with elaborate undulations.
It was hued just for me.

Why did
you abandon me
and leave the
seamless germ
to remind me of you?

It
dares me,
as it sits there
mirroring messages
as rotund as its bulk,
to recall how
with wild abandon
we reeled in unison
with the ovation
of the egg.

As light
as the bulk it upends
we whirled
on tiptoe,
pivoted,
and with lusty energy
lunged across the grass
to grasp
the elusive football.

**As melodic
as the oration
it chants
we toe-tapped
the beach rocks
in excessive exclamations
to catch the spout
of the clam
before we could
catch his breath.**

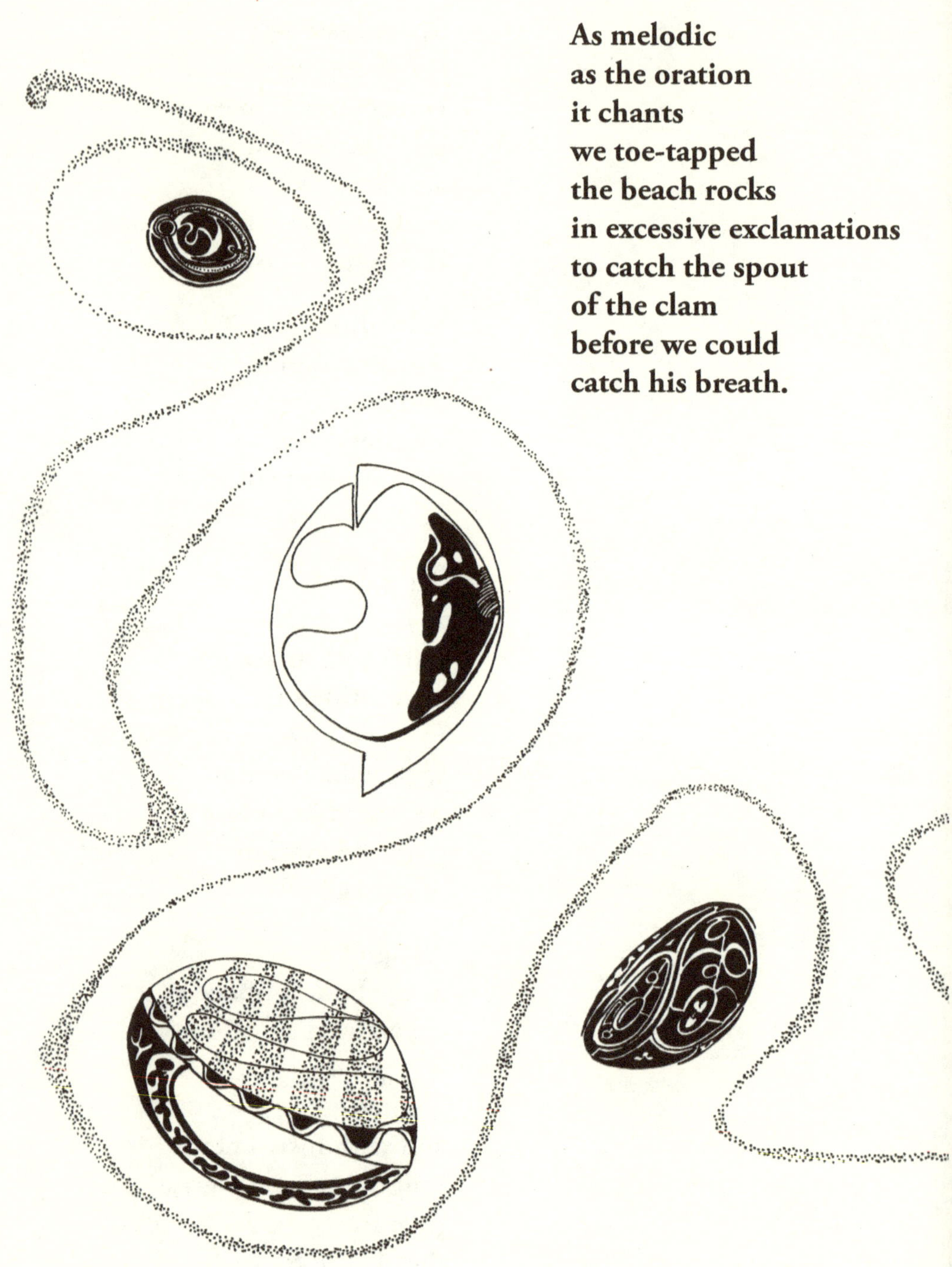

Buoyed by the
echo
of those jaunts
I pick up
the egg
with swift gesture
to cherish
once again
its shurring lullaby
only to find
it has grown hard
and rattles the edges
into cracks.

Why did
you abandon me
and leave the now
seamed germ
to remind me of you?

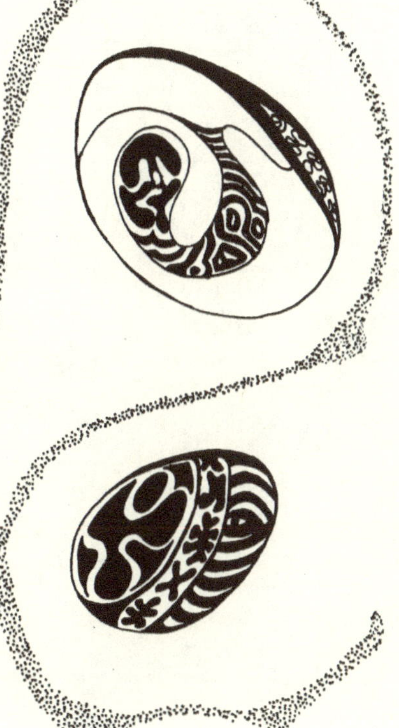

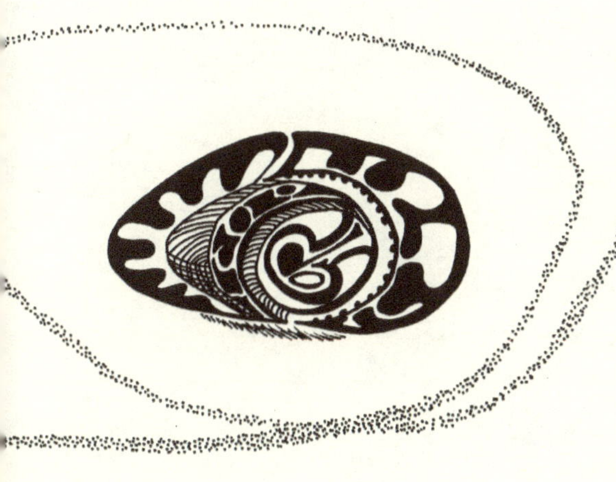

Love American Style

The golden strands
    the real thing
Curl like a long drag of smoke
    the real thing
Around an empty face
    the re-vealed thing
Free-floating, dusky—
One eye spots YOU, JUST YOU
    as the real thing
While the other eye—bold, painted—
Is cruisin' for GUYS—ALL YOU GUYS—
    for the real thing
And the lips, painted into
A crimson heart for kissing
    you, real thing
Invite you and you and you and you
    things, real, really real
To a flower party
    for love, American style
On dew-misted, never-never water
    in Ameri- can style
With menthol KOOL-filtered people
    American style
Perfectly paired
    and in love, American style

Hang the banner!!!
Hang the banner!!!
For LOVE AMERICAN STYLE
IT'S THE REAL THING

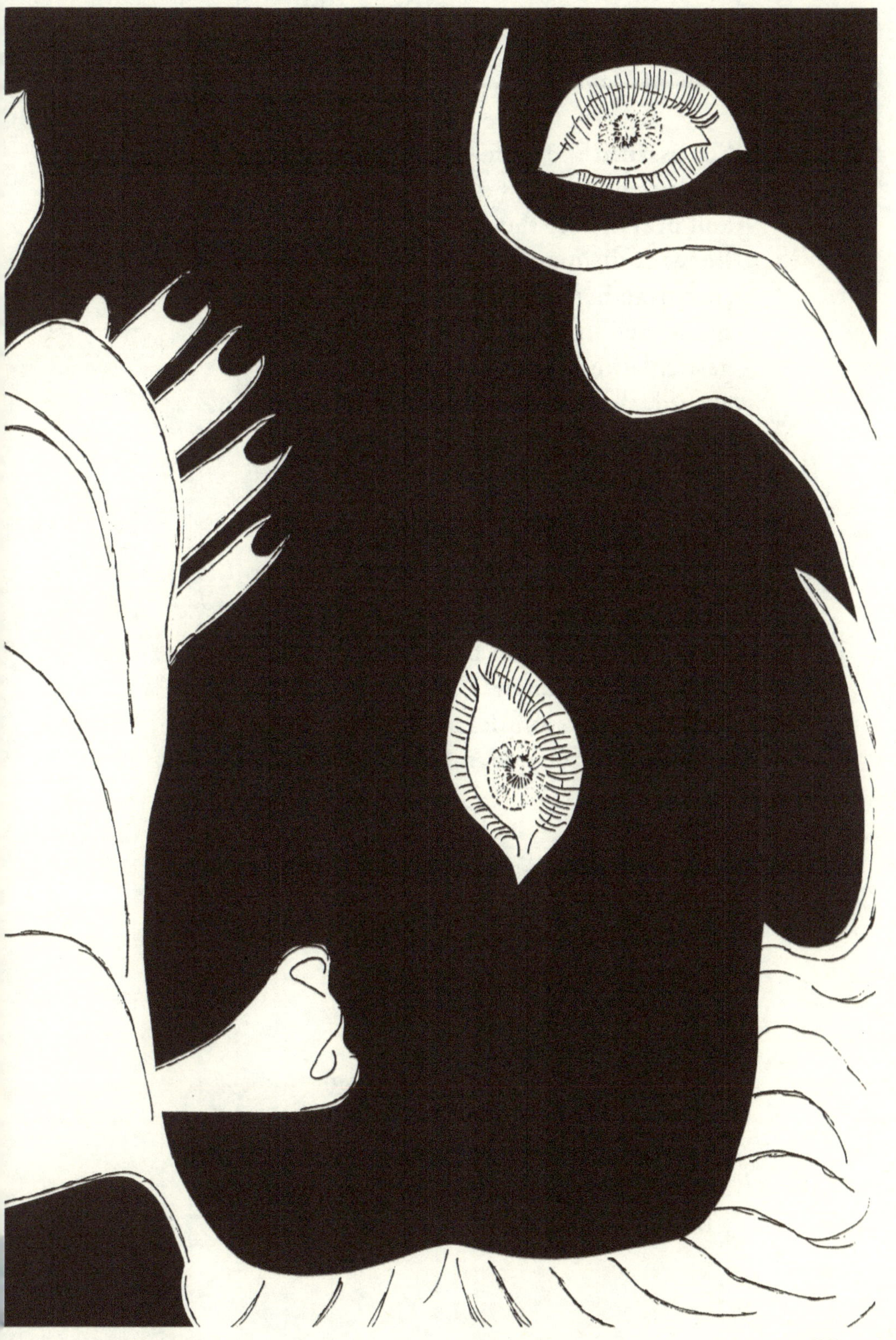

Edge of Daylight

She assailed the path—
appetite bundled in rage—
and peered over the edge.
Beneath the outcropping
succoring her toes, the
sea argued in rabid
gesticulations—mockingly
absurd, she speculated—
as it breathed in sinuous
jade tapestries and churned
out shirred scum. What fable
are you straining through
your colander of sand?
Like children twisting into
snow angels, are you beguiling
Hades in a debonair
backstroke of granules
antiseptically choreographed?

Inside the house, he lay
there pensively, her son of
thirteen, who had cancer. He
scrutinized the edge of daylight.
Posturing easterly, loose clouds
groped obscurely, portending the
evening a look of denial.
"No dungeons tonight?" she asked.
"The tumor is growing," he knew.
She embraced the comforter at
his feet, bunching it into
a bouffant of anguish.

"Want to talk to the doctor?" she softened.
He sighed querulously, "Why did it come
back?"
"I know; it's not something we can settle."
"I'm not afraid. There are just so many sounds
I would still like to measure," he pondered.
"Would you like to give it to someone else?"
"No, I've grown into it," he owned
absolving the night its ebony taste.

Later, in the fog diffusing
the mirth of the seals,
she found her nemesis—
his fertile spirit shrouding
her in an unquenchable sob.

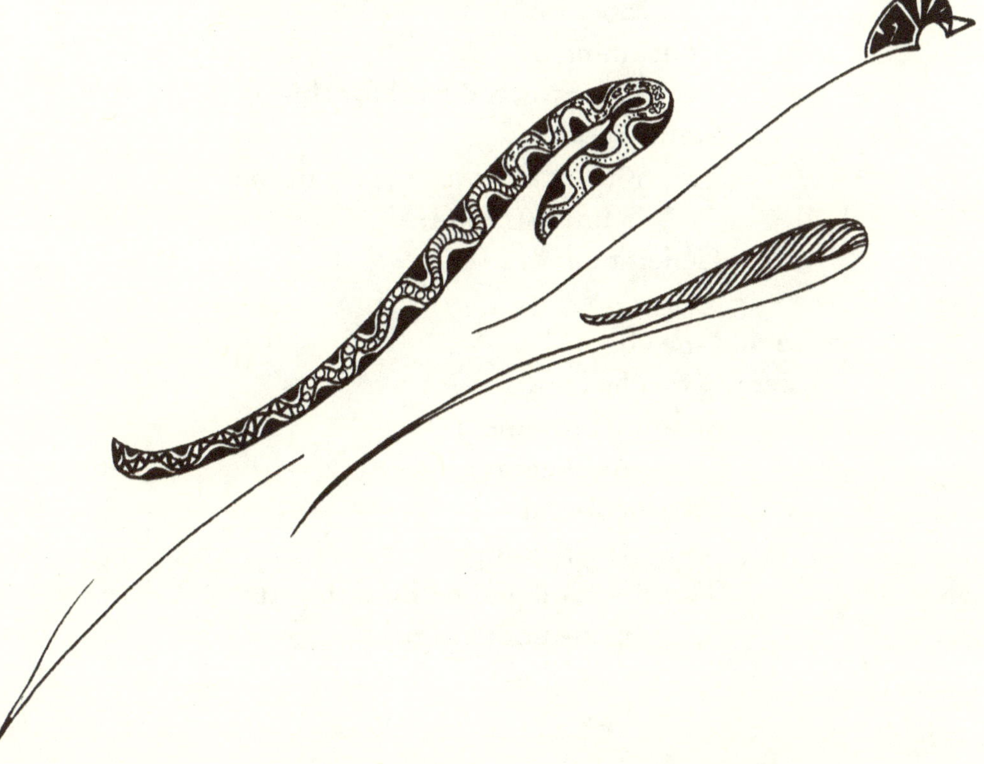

Communication

He talked to me today
of smoking marijuana

He of the eighteen-year-old
        Raging
                (A bequest of war)
        Hating
                (A system of no recourse)
        Hawking
                (A self)
        World

Me of the forty-year-old
        Placating
                ("There's not much we can do
                about it")
        Consuming
                ("We worked hard for this")
        Status-seeking
                ("Now that we are part of the
                administration…")
        Generation

He told me about
listening to a leaf unfold
        Snailing movement
                (Awakening)
        Pristine sound
                (Hearkening)
        Timid wedding of embryo to earth
                (Consummating)

I told him about
seeing a dandelion seed
        Dying yellow
                (Contemplating)
        Jutting spokes
                (Answering)
        Whitened globule stayed by the sun
                (Communing)

We talked about
touching a caterpillar
        Soft creeping
                (Birth is)
        Hard encasement
                (Life has)
        Liberated flight joining colored
        motion to immutable time
                (Death will be)

Childhood Nunnery

I didn't like to visit her.
It was like spying on God
or living a surreal fairy tale.
Once a month, my mother went to see
her, the sister who had been a nun
longer than my mother had been alive.

Trepid-footing the oak grove with its
scraggly-lichened tresses and
high-stepping myself up ivy-bearded stairs
angling onto a heavily bolted door
caused me to wonder whether I was
stone-marking in Hansel and Gretel's
wood-brier or boosting myself into the
clabbered air of Rapunzel's tower.

The doorbell's chant intoned from
the bowels of the convent and eventually
a climbing foot-tattoo came down the hall
ushering us into the sterile interior.
Anchored by my mother's strength—and skirt—
I was propelled down the long corridor in tempo
to the black creature luring me onward.

On the other side of what seemed like a
journey through Alice's rabbit hole, I
found myself trying not to stare at towering,
wood-shuttered windows, bleached daddy-
long-legged walls, and lights that screwed
into candlesticks. There, beside a gigantic
cross with a dead Jesus, I sat waiting
for the "hush" to come down the hall.

I tried to talk to my family staring in silence,
but words denuded me; they came out in
scato-patter that sounded like sins
ricocheting across the walls. I attempted to
distract myself by looking out the window,
but the real world was so far down there.

Trundled in black, there she was with
only her face and hands showing—
tentative smile...rosebud lips...
gold-rimmed glasses...genteel
eyes...delicate hands reaching....
She inquired and we recited:
yes, worked in hot sun in fields all summer,
yes, walked home down highway,
yes, older sister driving but had no extra car,
yes, said rosary together every night.

Satisfied that we were working for God,
she led us from "the tower" giving us a
soliloquy on His love. As her eyes rolled inside
her head, I puzzled whether my eyes would get
caught on the back side as I practiced
the art. She was not like her parents who had
crossed days of water to live in a new land where
they had embraced the unknown buttressed on one
side by war and on the other by displacement.

I knew when I spurted from the woods,
in guise of Red Riding Hood,
that I would return to hear
how, like Ashenputtel, my aunt, daily,
dutifully, climbed winding, rickety stairs
to comb the tresses of her sick sisters.

Plant Matters

I tried to engage him
I needed to talk in plantglyphics with him
I knew he understood the linguistics of a gardener
        ...how the wind mimics
        each shift   of a bud
            breaking...how you clutch
                your breath in soil
        squeezed   from clod...how
                the gusto of worm   angling
            teases seeds

He didn't appear today
Instead, a tall replica of him
carefully, oh, so carefully—
for two days—scrubbed
the view facing my way
On the third day—mid-day—
housecoat seed-podding him
he waddled to the gate and
studied his garden the way
you absorb sun in cold-bone time
Unable, seemingly, to see forever
he searched some more, flashlight
dancing with the twittering leaves

She asked me what I wanted my legacy to be
No answer surfaced; I thought I had lived
my legacy. Didn't she know that the eyeshot
that answered his stare was the flame of my giving

Sea Sway

Leaning on
the shadow day
had passed through,
the sea shivered
at the lips of my love,
and, frilling shamelessly,
he owned me.
Repeatedly,
yielding me to the limbus,
then, bending me back again,
he turned himself
downforwardonto…pulling
…drawing…restraining…
enclosing. Finally,
lassoing the crest—breath
abeyant—he surfed the
undertow and caught me
in a water jacket that
powdered
the beach with sand shine.

Afterward, there we lay,
gossamer and sway,
ready to bulk up
again
to the shape
of our love.

QUIVERING ON THE INSIDE

The Four Wheelers

shaped the
dust as they owned the winds
come calling from across the
Santa Lucias to this Eden east.
Here, convolutions of land swirled
in ever-recurring themes of time.
A lone electrical pole denied by the
windmill gods, stopped in mid-climb
while jostling nature into circuitry.
The oaks, long ago conceived in bowels
of motion, crawled along the ground
with coarse, growling barks and stooped
intermittently to anchor arms in their
rise from squattage to perfect umbrellas.
Other oaks, arthritic appendages gnarling,
bent their butts backwards up the ravines
like a bevy of dirndl skirts curtsying.
Buckeye, warts many-eyed, glared
from hog-wild reaches of leaf roll.
From beneath, pewter rabbits, skittish-stepping,
wide-eyed the interlopers in their machine cages.
Blobs of hoary fog spit against the hillsides
hag-nagging sustenance from neighbor-ocean.
A quilled thistle, loaf-bread-bosomed,
spoke of its July untwining…mute.

And, the four wheelers, where are they?
In ever-recurring themes of growling and
stooping and gnarling and butt-reaching,
they squatted into perfect umbrellas
and were shaped by the wind
into the motion of silence gone wild.

Bread Baking

Giving too generously
is a hunger that one cannot
satisfy with unleavened bread.
It takes fermenting yeast
pummeled to a kneading
and rising crescendo
of resilient flesh
stretched abundantly,
like my mother's bosom,
into voluptuous mounds
of bread-loaf opulence.

Can such a cadenced dance
of feverish mass
be contained in aluminum pans
of rectangular means?

A Conundrum?

my loving you in
quick intakes of breath
wheezing through the narrow
passage of sky drawn
back into a curtain
of blood

you didn't take me
into the pasture of
sky swinging hands full
of songs in gestures
of tender epiphany

neither did you offer
me flower chains of
forget-me-nots strung
on whispers vibrating
to spider thread

nor did you translate for
me the sighing of
bird wings knotting
pansy beds into
an epigraph trailing with
feather kisses

instead
unyielding to soft
spokes of dandelion silk
shimmering in your path
you slipped into
the a-rhythmical beat of a
crippled hawk grasping
the crimson scent
of clutching despair

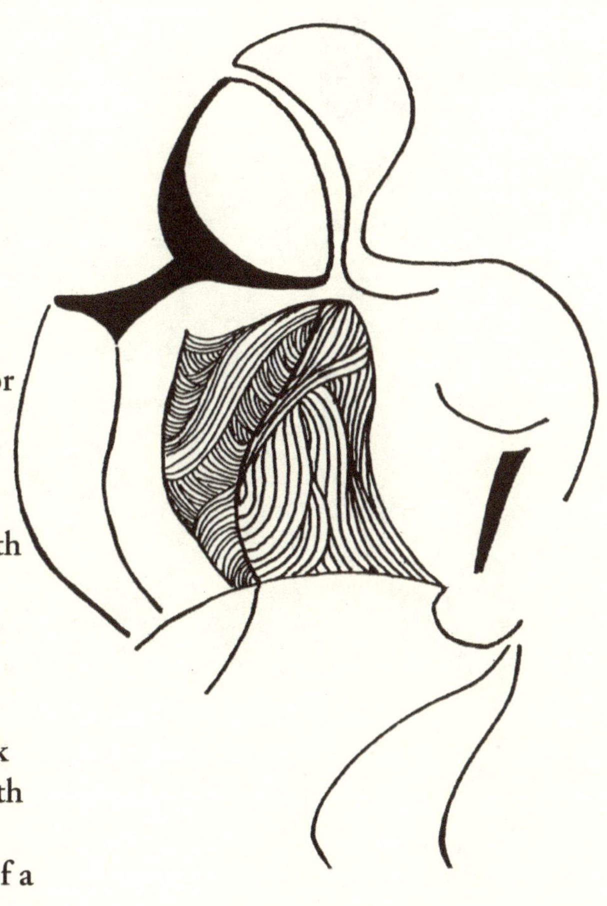

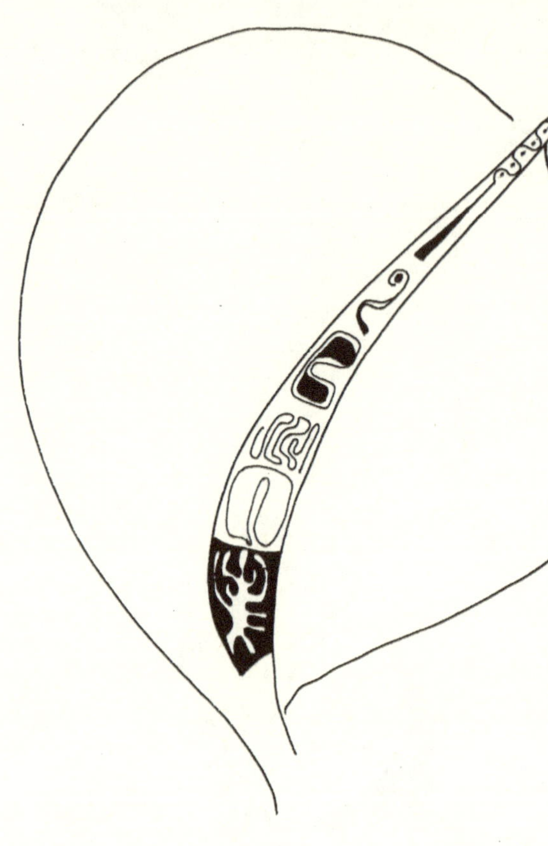

Breathe

Whimsical designs
in tonal over-dye
moon the sky
as the boys blow
expansive bubbles
into the ocean pretending
the turmoil of their
breached lives
will not roil Sky Belly.
Anguish, this moment,
is claimed by
the susurrous bubble
top-lofting.
Unable to handle its
shape, it obeys
oblivion when tagged
by sky dust.

Across the parking lot,
an infant suckles
breast. Hold on.
Your susurrous bubble,
also wambling, is
anchored for now.
Inhale vigorously, weaning
is not your pome.

Point of View

When I visited you yesterday,
you whispered to me,
liquid breath coming in jagged rhythm,
that the peach tree, this year,
was leaving a trail of crushed petals.
Your arms,
in flattened silence,
held no buoyant promise
for another spring.
My arms,
voluptuously echoing ornamental dreams,
felt strangeness in you.
At home,
watching the crows
hunkering the wind,
my rhythm came in vibrant breath.

What do you see—
you who say
the electric wires obstruct my view?
…those wires I never saw
until your saying placed them there….
They? …the life lines
the crows draw along behind their bodies.

Real Fantasy

The child sat composed

Music smothered the air

A clown materialized—
regalia spewed from cavernous
mouths of decoration
Billowing swaths of cloth
disguised lean bones

Head hidden by
an upward flounce of his arm
he waited for his note
frenzied...raucous...brassy
He catapulted
across the stage
pumping his movements into
a chaos of abandonment
harsh...glaring...discordant

Cheers riveted the air

A face...a face—
bulbous and smudged—
stared from the stage
and nodded in empty curtsy

Tears pooled in
the crevices of his cheeks

A closer look at the clown

From those pools of tears
rivulets were
now
jetting to
the saw of the sobs

Uproarious applause

The hands in the child's
lap were numbed into
stillness
Those were her embellishments
he was wearing
She spoke vehemently,
vehemently, vehemently, VEHEMENTLY
Gibberish chained her words
She reached
to claim her
possessions...her
arms dismembered

She looked
down
into
herself
She...the clown
frozen in verisimilitude

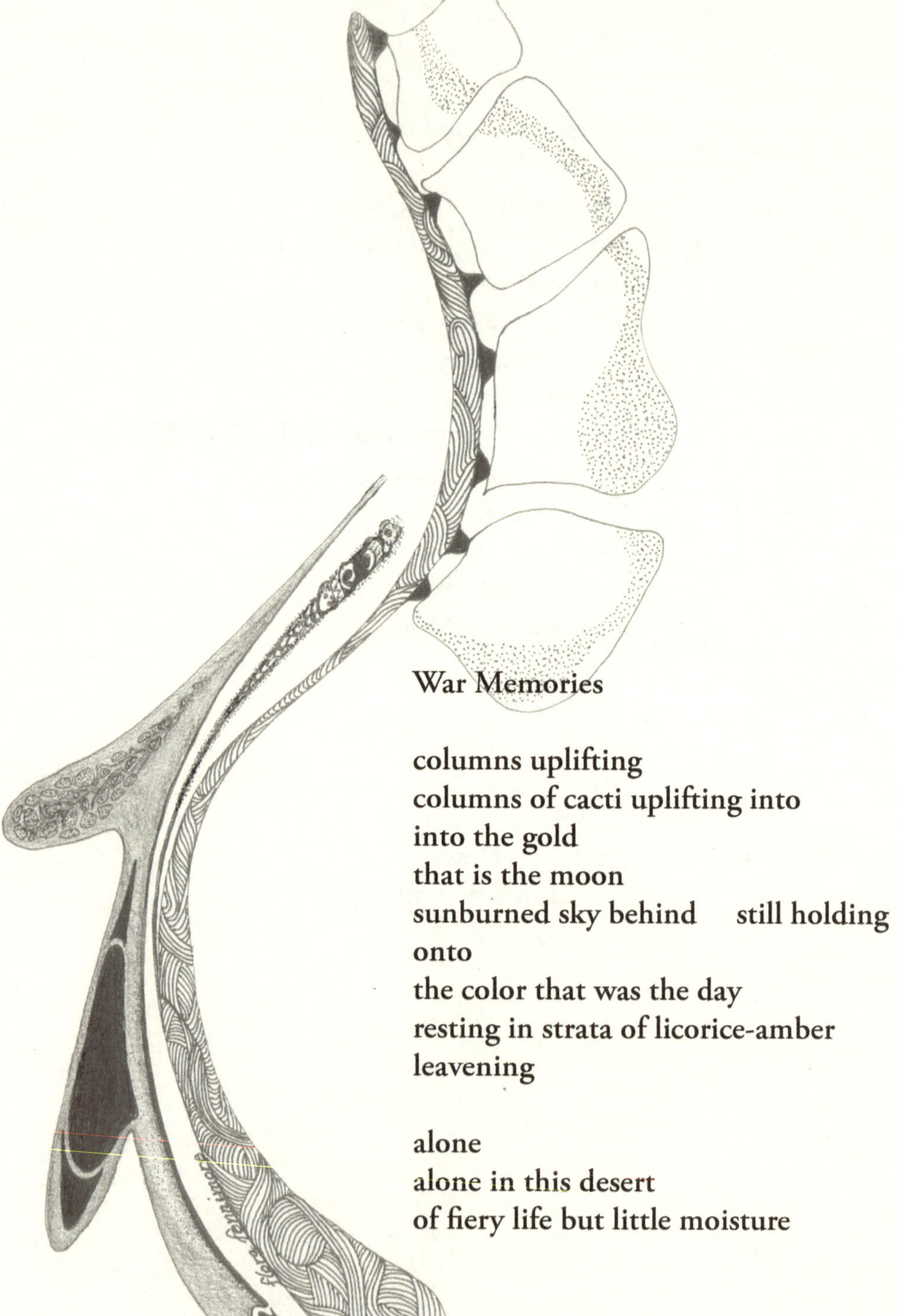

War Memories

columns uplifting
columns of cacti uplifting into
into the gold
that is the moon
sunburned sky behind   still holding
onto
the color that was the day
resting in strata of licorice-amber
leavening

alone
alone in this desert
of fiery life but little moisture

reflecting on the soldier
talking...crying
"the enemy angel—
I don't know how
to get him out of my mind"
his crying could not bring him back
"they don't know what they took from us!"

alone
alone in this desert
day moves into day
even as the columns of cacti
suck hoarsely for water

focusing on the elderly woman
bartering her rosary beads
talking...crying
"I spent my nights crying my fear"
she, threshing the bed and
twisting her hair into sore spots,
could not bring back her childhood
"I don't know how to get
myself out of my mind
they don't know what they took from us!"

light going into night
the desert
seeming serenity in arid spaces
life fighting for itself

the blame of shame   or
the shame of blame?

Night Offering

As the wind reeled southward
Flailing its shroud in obscure gestures
A suppressed fragment ignited
Eddied in gossamer swirls
And, startlingly, offered the night

an orb
of heady orange

A moon becoming,
For a carnelian moment,
Was

Then, gently withdrawing from
roundness
It yielded to the striations
Of the bay's breath
Divested the night of darkness
And diffused its radiance into

a silence
of voluminous rouge

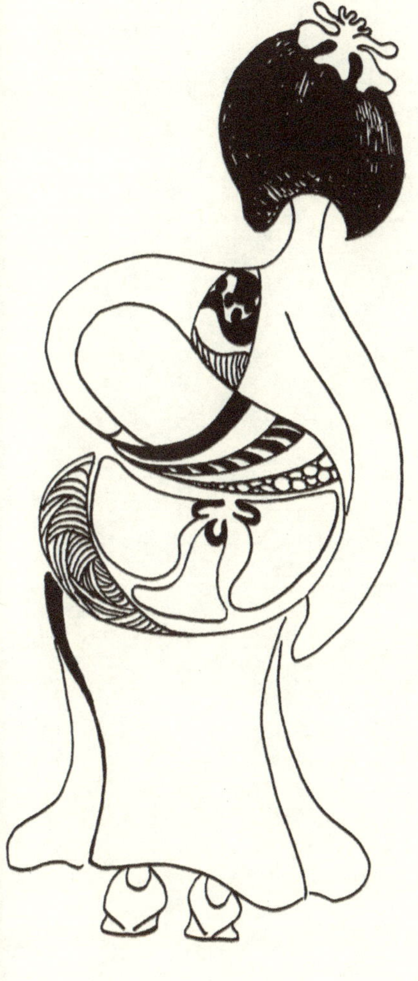

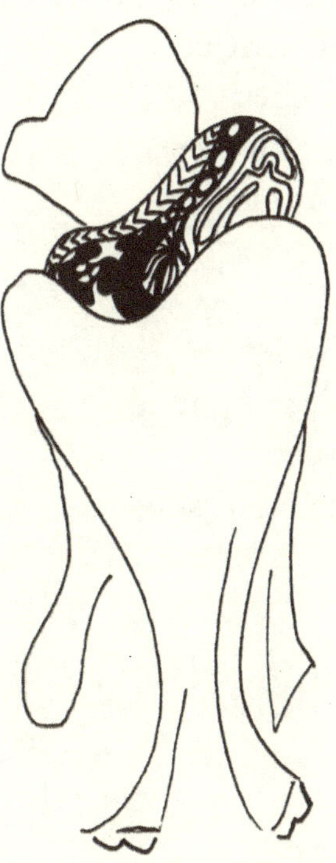

Adieu

The leaves
leave not
They leaf lightly into a swirl
leaving me
circling

They a-swirl sprightly
into a leaving
leaving me
twirling
    in fall-ing wonder
    at the persistence
    of continuity

In their leaf-leaving
they nimbly lay down a
parch(ment)ed
rain-etched
dance of leaves
jettisoning

Hush!
They've left
their leaving in a
leaf-filled
scattering of silence

Peer into the once-flutter
Look...lean in,
eye-rhyme unstated...
at blight, rust, scabbing, decay
gathered into a rendering of
brackish eye sockets
stained lips, scaled ears—
the faces of the dead—
each a memory restated

This blaze of remains
a-stirringly
still dances the
rhythm of the universe
waiting for the
next
leaf-leaving

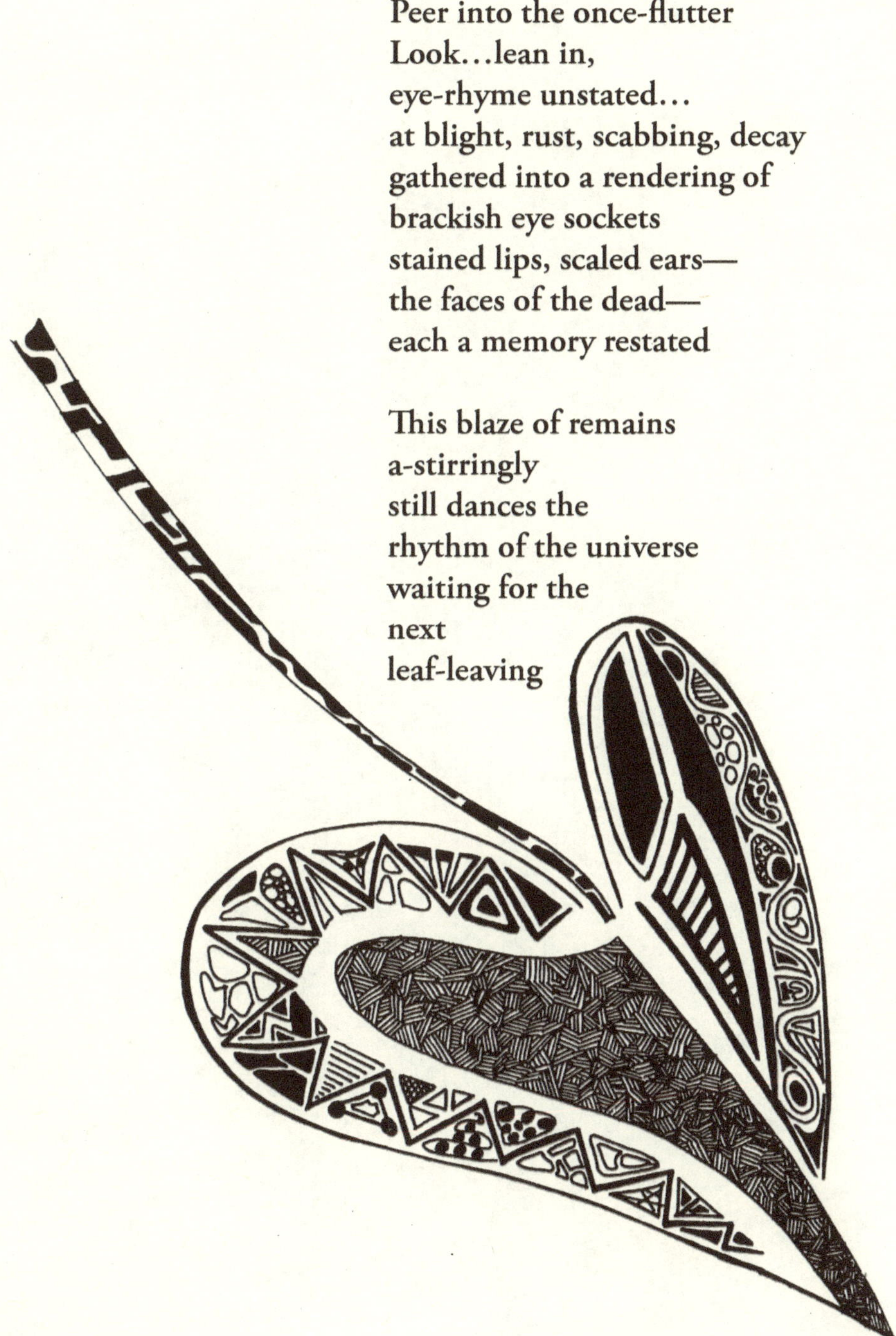

FLORA FENNIMORE

has written all of her life. In fact, her primary possession is paper—paper on which she wrote and illustrated articles, stories, poetry, and books; paper on which her elementary, secondary, and university students recorded their unique feelings; and paper on which writers throughout the ages brought their worlds into hers.

Believing passionately that man's greatest gift is his ability to create, Flora Fennimore designed many original programs in writing and other expressive arts which she shared with teachers and students locally and nationally. She has just completed a book for teachers of university students entitled *Writing: Writing Really is Talking in New Gestures.*

A native of the Northwest, Flora Fennimore has lived primarily on the West Coast and in England. She is now finding new facets of nature's whisperings through country living in Monterey County, California, where she resides with her husband, Ed. She is a professor emeritus of Western Washington University, Bellingham, Washington, where she taught writing and expressive arts for nearly 30 years.

www.ingramcontent.com/pod-product-compliance
Lightning Source LLC
LaVergne TN
LVHW050944080826
845145LV00004B/1411

* 9 7 8 0 9 6 1 9 4 0 7 1 3 *